ERIC LINDROS
POWER PLAYER

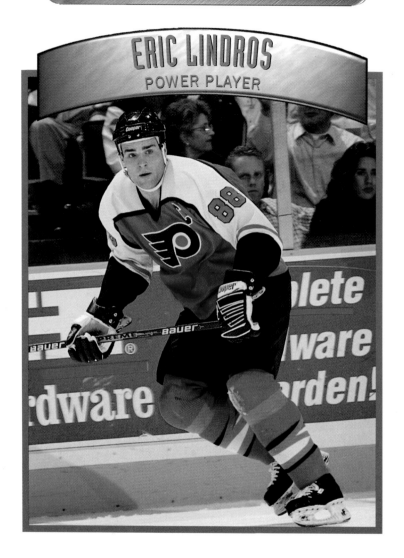

BY MARK STEWART

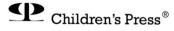

Children's Press®
A Division of Grolier Publishing
New York London Hong Kong Sydney
Danbury, Connecticut

Photo Credits

Cover, Allsport USA: 36 right ©(Robert LaBerge), 27; AP/Wide World
Photos: 30, 34, 35, 38; ©Bruce Bennet Studios: 22 ©(G. Bennet), 33, 37,
47 (J. Giamundo), 6, 45 top right (Brian Winkler), 32; Reuters/Corbis-
Bettmann: 28, 45 top left; Rocky Widner: 3, 24, 36 left, 38 inset, 43;
SportsChrome: 13, 46; Vantage Point/Dan Hamilton: 14, 17, 19, 23,
26, 44 top right.

Library of Congress Cataloging-in-Publication Data

Stewart, Mark.
      Eric Lindros : power player / by Mark Stewart.
         p.   cm. — (Sports stars)
      Summary: A biography of the physical Canadian-born hockey player
who played on the Canadian Olympic team in 1992, but whose career
in the National Hockey League had a rocky beginning, before he was
signed by the Philadelphia Flyers.
      ISBN 0-516-20487-4 (lib.bdg.)   0-516-26052-9 (pbk.)
      1. Lindros, Eric—Juvenile literature. 2. Hockey players—Canada—
Biography—Juvenile literature. [1. Lindros, Eric. 2. Hockey players.]
1. Title. II. Series.
GV848.5.L56S84   1997
796.962'092
[B]—DC21   96-39587
                                              CIP
                                              AC

CONTENTS

CHAPTER 1
Power and Grace 7

CHAPTER 2
Born to Skate 8

CHAPTER 3
A Difficult Beginning 21

CHAPTER 4
Free at Last 31

CHAPTER 5
Fulfilling the Promise 37

Chronology 44

Career Statistics 47

About the Author 48

★ 1 ★

POWER AND GRACE

Philadelphia Flyers forward Eric Lindros guides the puck up ice, gaining speed as he glides over the center line. Attracting two opponents, he makes a crisp pass to a teammate. Then, in a sudden burst of energy, Lindros knocks aside one defender and breaks out into open ice. His teammate returns the puck to him. In a blur of motion, Lindros flicks a shot that streaks past the goaltender and into the back of the net. As Eric, his teammates, and the fans celebrate, the defenders shake their heads. Never, in the history of the NHL, has one player possessed so much power and strength, combined with so much grace and speed.

★ 2 ★

BORN TO SKATE

Eric's athletic ability appeared at an early age. When other children were still riding tricycles, Eric Lindros was on a two-wheeler. When other kids were just learning how to swim, he was already waterskiing. So no one was surprised when, a year or so after Eric laced up his first pair of hockey skates, he was shooting, passing, and stickhandling as well as players twice his age. Eric's parents decided early on to support and encourage him in whatever he wanted to do. To their great delight, Eric excelled at nearly everything he tried.

Eric was born to play hockey.

Eric in a school picture when he was five

★ ★ ★

Although Eric's parents loved sports, they understood the importance of an education. They made sure that Eric, his brother, Brett, and his sister, Robin, put as much effort into their schoolwork as they did into their sports. The rule in the Lindros house was simple: finish your homework before you play, and keep your grades up—or else.

Eric liked math best, but he did well in almost all of his subjects. He did not do as well, however, when it came to making friends. Eric could be very shy, yet also very competitive. The other children did not always understand him, so he was not a very popular boy. Eric tried to make other children notice and respect him by doing better than they did on tests and special projects. This approach did not win him many friends, but it did well for his grades.

"It wasn't that I studied that hard," Eric claims, "it was more a matter of making sure I did all my work. School's not difficult, unless you don't pay attention to what's going on in your class. If you do listen and you're still having problems, then it's time to ask questions. People are so worried about how they look and acting cool in school that they forget why they're there."

Eric and his brother learned to play hockey on a rink their father created each winter behind the family's home in London, a city in the Canadian province of Ontario. Each night, after practicing with the boys, Eric's father would hose down the surface. The next morning, the ice would be as smooth as glass. "We worked on a lot of passing, one-time shots, tons of deflections," Eric recalls. "Our favorite drill was 'skate in a circle.' I would skate the circle, take a pass, and shoot as quickly as possible on net. Then my dad would get lined up to do the same thing, and I would pass to him. So I'd get my passing in. We'd have a great time."

Eric watches a play develop and waits for his chance.

Eric attracted national attention while playing for the Metro Toronto Junior League.

———————— ★ ★ ★ ————————

Eric also did a lot of practicing on his own. He would work for hours on every part of his game, sometimes spending entire days on the ice. Eric imagined himself skating in front of huge, cheering crowds, and he played heavy-metal music on his tape player to keep him pumped up. "With all the snow banked around the rink, the music echoed all over the backyard," he says. "It was just like a concert. I thought it was great, though the neighbors probably didn't share my view!"

After moving to Toronto, Ontario, Eric really blossomed in its youth hockey league. He seemed to see and understand things on the ice that other boys his age did not. Around the age of 13 or 14, Eric began to grow faster than the other boys, too. Soon, he looked and played like someone who was 16 or 17.

In 1989, at age 16, Eric was the first player selected in the Ontario Hockey League (OHL) draft. It had always been his dream to play in the OHL, but the team that selected him—the Sault St. Marie Greyhounds—played hundreds of miles from his home. Eric did not like the idea of living so far away. He would miss his family. And because the team spent so much time traveling, there was a possibility that he would not graduate from high school on time. His parents asked the Greyhounds to trade their son, but the rules were clear: first draft picks were not allowed to be traded. Besides, who did the Lindroses think they were, trying to push the league around? "Take it or leave it," replied the OHL Board of Governors. Eric and his parents decided to "leave it." He went to live with a family in suburban Detroit, and he signed up to play in the North American Hockey League.

Just as he had in Toronto's Junior League, Eric excelled in the
North American Hockey League in Detroit.

★ ★ ★

After playing just 14 games for Detroit
Compuware, Eric had racked up 24 goals and
29 assists. Canadian hockey fans were very
angry. They did not understand why the OHL
would let their country's finest teenage player—
a player who many believed was already good
enough to start in the NHL at the age of 16—
just walk away. Eric also led the Canadian Junior
Team to the world championships in Finland. By
midseason, the OHL rewrote its rules, and Eric
was traded to the Oshawa Generals for $60,000
and three players. Oshawa was much closer to
the Lindros home in Toronto, so Eric agreed to
return to the OHL and play. "The experience in
Detroit made me mature quickly," says Eric of
his brief stay in the United States. "It's different
when your mom's not there to take care of
everything for you. I think I gained a lot of
independence while I was there and it helped
me get used to living away from home."

Under pressure from angry hockey fans, the OHL allowed Eric to join the Oshawa Generals.

By this time, Eric was approaching his full height and weight. At 6' 4" and 227 pounds, he scattered other players like bowling pins, and he answered with his fists when older, more experienced players tried to bully him. As the 1991 NHL draft approached, there was no doubt in anyone's mind who the number-one pick would be. All that remained to be seen was which team would get Eric.

★ 3 ★

A DIFFICULT BEGINNING

The Quebec Nordiques stumbled through the 1990–91 season with the worst record in the National Hockey League. The team finished out of the playoffs for the fourth year in a row. The Nordiques desperately needed a superstar to turn the team around and lure fans back into their arena. Eric seemed to be the perfect player to do it. There was just one problem: Eric did not want to play for Quebec.

There were a number of reasons why the Nordiques did not make sense for Eric. The team's owner, Marcel Aubut, seemed unable to put a good team on the ice. The city of Quebec was also far away from the cities in the rest of

Quebec Nordiques owner Marcel Aubut

league. Eric hoped to make large amounts of
money doing commercials and selling products.
Playing in Quebec would have made it difficult
for Eric to accomplish this. The Nordiques,
themselves, were short on cash, and much
of what they could afford to pay Eric would
be eaten up by Quebec's high taxes.

The Lindroses let Aubut know their feelings, and they suggested that he trade Eric for a package of players, draft picks, and cash that might turn the team around. Aubut ignored them, and Quebec selected Eric on draft day. Nordique fans were outraged when Eric refused

Eric and his brother watch anxiously as Eric is drafted by the Nordiques.

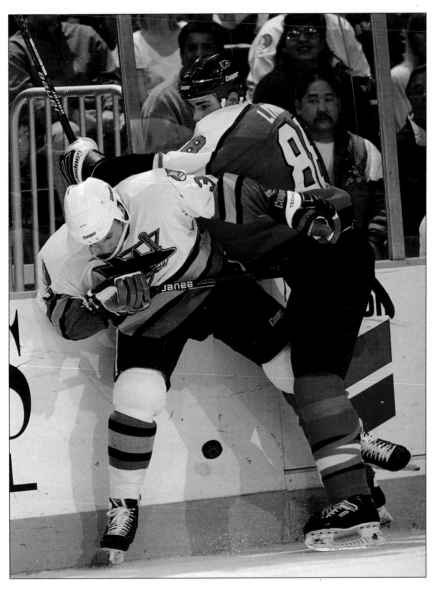

Just as he refuses to back down on the ice, Eric refused to back down to the Nordiques.

to wear the team's jersey for publicity photos. They considered it a slap in the face. But Eric had his reasons. "I took a lot of flak for not putting the Nordiques sweater on," he says, "but I think wearing the sweater would have been a false statement. I didn't want to misguide people as to my true feelings."

That night, Eric and his brother, Brett, shared a cab back to their hotel. Eric sat silently, wondering how the biggest day of his life had turned out to be so bad. Then he burst into tears.

Eric offered to play for the Nordiques if they promised to trade him after two seasons. The team refused, stating that they wanted him for life. "All I could picture was me wearing prison stripes," he laughs. The next few months were the most difficult of Eric's young life. He turned down a reported $50 million offer from the Nordiques and decided to play elsewhere for no salary.

After refusing to play with the Nordiques, Eric played for the Canadian National Team in the 1992 Olympics.

Eric's plan was simple. He would stand his ground until the Nordiques traded him, or wait two years until their rights to him expired and then reenter the draft. He might have nothing to show for all his years of hard work and practice, but Quebec's owner would have nothing to show for his number-one draft choice. Eric believed that Aubut would give in before he did.

Eric could never have handled such pressure without the help of his family. "My family has backed me from day one," he says. "The way I see it, you're only as good as your family—I'm a

Eric could not have made it to Philadelphia without the support of his family.

Eric tries on a Philadelphia jersey for the first time.

product of the values my family gave me. I was raised to believe in hard work, because if you worked hard—at school, at sports, at your job— you'd have more choices."

On June 30, 1992, the Quebec Nordiques finally decided to let Eric go. They held an "auction" for the young superstar, and the Philadelphia Flyers were the winners. In return for Eric, the Flyers parted with stars Mike Ricci, Ron Hextall, and Peter Forsberg, as well as three more players, two first-round picks, and $15 million in cash. Never before had a single athlete commanded such a price. Never before had a rookie been under the pressure Eric would soon face.

Eric celebrates after scoring a goal.

★ 4 ★

FREE AT LAST

After sitting out for a year, Eric Lindros could hardly wait to play his first NHL game. Wearing number 88 for the Philadelphia Flyers, he took the ice against the defending league champion Pittsburgh Penguins and scored a goal. In his next game, against the New Jersey Devils, Eric scored again! In all, he netted 41 goals that first season, even though he missed 23 games with a knee injury.

How valuable was Philadelphia's rookie sensation? When Eric did not play, Philadelphia won just seven times; when he played, the team went 29–23–9. Eric drew huge crowds wherever the Flyers played, including the crowd that came to boo him when the team skated in Quebec. Still

Quebec fans make fun of Eric upon his return as a Flyer.

feeling the sting of Eric's refusal to play for their
beloved Nordiques, the fans hurled plastic bottles
and pacifiers onto the ice. It was their way of
calling Eric a baby.

In his second year with the Flyers, Eric really
developed a feel for the pro game. He scored 44
goals and added 53 assists, and he played in his
first All-Star Game.

Eric skates for the Eastern Conference in the 1994 NHL All-Star Game.

By the end of that 1993–94 season, Eric had begun to notice something very important. Thanks to his size, aggressiveness, and fine stickwork, he could dominate a hockey game without registering a goal or an assist. No one wanted to tangle with him in the corners or along

Eric checks an opposing player over the boards.

the boards, and even the league's biggest defensemen backed off a little when he came swooping into the offensive zone. In other words, Eric did not have to skate all over the ice smashing into people—he just had to scare them into thinking he might. Eric could shake up opponents by doing little more than floating around the ice. And with one eye fixed on number 88, a defender could easily lose sight of his man, which created great scoring opportunities for Eric's teammates.

No one benefited more from Eric's presence than left wing John LeClair, who joined the Flyers in February 1994 after a trade with the Montreal Canadiens. With defenders so worried about Eric, LeClair was free to practice his specialty: scooping up loose pucks and scoring. In his first season with the Flyers, LeClair scored 25 goals in just 37 games. In his second season, he found the net 51 times to lead the team. On Eric's right, Mikael Renberg blossomed, too. A talented

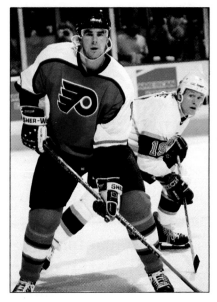

John LeClair   Mikael Renberg

all-around player from Sweden, Renberg
narrowly missed winning the Calder Trophy
as the NHL's top rookie in 1994.

The line of Lindros, LeClair, and Renberg
soon became known as the "Legion of Doom."
Each player stood well over 6' 2" and weighed
between 215 and 225 pounds—quite large, by
hockey standards. The sight of these three
brutes barreling down the ice was enough to
make a goaltender consider early retirement!

⭐ 5 ⭐

FULFILLING THE PROMISE

The 1994–95 season was a special one for Eric. It had been seven long years since the Flyers had won more games than they lost, and fans at the Philadelphia Spectrum wanted to root for a winner. Eric was named team captain, and he vowed to deliver. The role of leader was new for Eric, who as a kid was usually the youngest

In 1994, Eric first wore a "C" on his jersey when he became team captain.

player on his team. "I was a little surprised," he says of becoming an NHL captain at the ripe old age of 21.

Eric guided the team to a first-place finish in the tough Atlantic Division. Near the end of the season, Eric was injured when he fired a slap shot that hit New York Rangers defenseman Jeff Beukeboom and went right back into Eric's left eye. It was a weird, one-in-a-million accident, but it could not have come at a worse time. Eric was out in front in the race for the Art Ross Trophy as the NHL's top point scorer, but the injury caused him to miss the last few games of the season. Pittsburgh's Jaromir Jagr was able to pass him in goals, 32 to 29, and tie him for the league lead with a total of 70 points.

Eric did not reveal how serious his injury was at the time, but he now admits that doctors told him he came very close to losing the sight in his eye. Still, he was able to rejoin his teammates in time for a run at the Stanley Cup. Eric played well, but he was not his usual self, and Philadelphia ran into the New Jersey Devils and their red-hot goalie, Martin Brodeur. The Flyers fell in a wild six-game series to the team that eventually won the Stanley Cup. Eric was disappointed, but on balance, the season had been a good one.

A few weeks later, Eric was named the most valuable player in the NHL. He had fulfilled a lifetime of promise and expectations. Some were saying that he was ready to take his place among the sport's all-time greats, but Eric quickly put such notions into perspective. "If you start

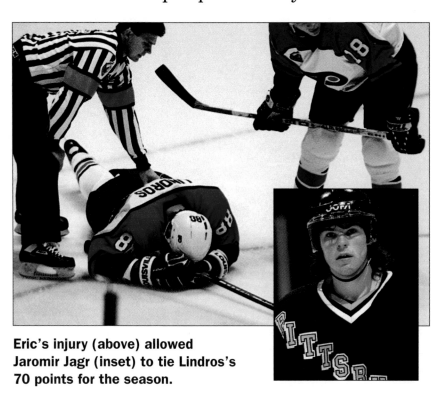

Eric's injury (above) allowed Jaromir Jagr (inset) to tie Lindros's 70 points for the season.

believing along those lines," he told reporters the night he accepted the Hart Trophy, "you might become satisfied. I certainly do not want to become satisfied with what I've done. I've got a lot of improving to do."

How much better can Eric Lindros get? As he learns more about himself and the game of hockey, he should be able to put his awesome skills to even better use. During the 1995–96 season, Eric took another important step forward, playing through a series of nagging injuries to top the 100-point mark for the first time in his pro career. If Eric can stand up to the poundings he receives each time he takes the ice, he may indeed prove to be one of the top players in NHL history.

Eric Lindros has learned that he can be a "power player" off the ice, too. Each summer, he gives his time to more than a dozen charity

Eric accepts the Hart Trophy as MVP of the league in 1994–95.

Eric signs autographs for excited children.

events, raising money and encouraging volun-
teers for everything from hospitals to sports
facilities. Eric's presence also has inspired others
to get involved. His pre-game dinners have done
wonders for Big Brothers/Big Sisters, attracting
many people to the program. Big Brothers/
Big Sisters provides role models for city kids
in the Philadelphia area. "There have been a lot
of good people who have helped me out over the
years—from doctors and nurses to coaches and
teachers. In some small way, I like to think I'm
helping those things to continue."

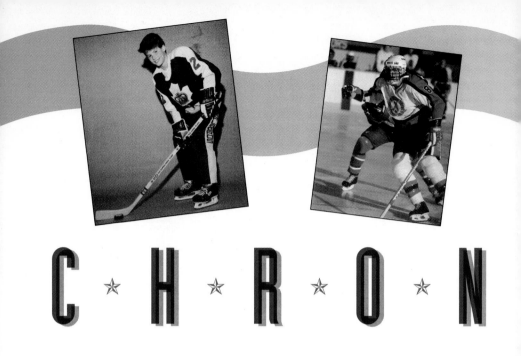

C ★ H ★ R ★ O ★ N

1973 • Eric is born in London, Ontario.

1989 • Eric moves to Detroit and plays for Detroit Compuware.

1990 • Eric leads the Canadian Junior National Team to the World Championships in Finland.
• Eric returns to Toronto and plays for the Oshawa Generals.

1991 • Although he does not want to play for Quebec, Eric is selected first in the NHL draft by the Quebec Nordiques. Eric refuses to play for the Quebec Nordiques during the 1991–92 season.

O ⋆ L ⋆ O ⋆ G ⋆ Y

1992   • Eric leads the Canadian Team to a silver medal in the Winter Olympics at Albertville, France.
   • In June, Quebec trades Eric to the Philadelphia Flyers for several players, cash, and two first-round draft picks.

1993–94 • Eric plays in his first NHL All-Star Game.

1994–95 • Eric wins the Hart Trophy as the NHL's most valuable player.

1995–96 • Eric records the first 100-point season of his career.

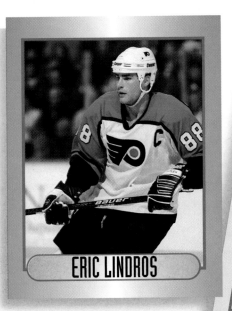

ERIC LINDROS

ERIC LINDROS

Place of Birth **London, Ontario**

Date of Birth **February 2, 1973**

Height **6' 4"**

Weight **229**

Pro Team **Philadelphia Flyers**

Canadian National Jr. Team **1990, 1991**

Canadian National Team **1992**

NHL All-Star **1994, 1995, 1996, 1997**

NHL Most Valuable Player **1995**

★ NHL STATISTICS ★

Season	Team	Games	Goals	Assists	Points
1992–93	Philadelphia	61	41	34	75
1993–94	Philadelphia	65	44	53	97
1994–95	Philadelphia	46	29	41	70*
1995–96	Philadelphia	73	47	68	115
1996–97	Philadelphia	52	32	47	79
Total (5 seasons)		**297**	**193**	**243**	**436**

*Tied for League Lead

ABOUT THE AUTHOR

Mark Stewart grew up in New York City in the 1960s and 1970s—when the Mets, Jets, and Knicks all had championship teams. As a child, Mark read everything about sports he could lay his hands on. Today, he is one of the busiest sportswriters around. Since 1990, he has written close to 500 sports stories for kids, including profiles on more than 200 atheletes, past and present. A graduate of Duke University, Mark served as senior editor of *Racquet,* a national tennis magazine, and was managing editor of *Super News,* a sporting goods industry newspaper. He is the author of Grolier's All-Pro Biography series, and four titles in the Children's Press Sports Stars series.